Carl Hiaasen was born and raised in Florida, where he still lives. He is a prize-winning journalist with a regular column in the *Miami Herald* and many articles in varied magazines. He started writing crime fiction in the early 1980s and he has also had several children's books and works of non-fiction published.

Roz Chast grew up in Brooklyn. In 1978, her cartoons began appearing in *The New Yorker*, where she has since published more than one thousand. She wrote and illustrated, most recently, *Going into Town;* the number one *New York Times* best seller *Can't We Talk About Something More Pleasant?*, a National Book Critics Circle Award and Kirkus Prize winner and a finalist for the National Book Award; *What I Hate: From A to Z;* and her cartoon collections *Theories of Everything* and *The Party, After You Left*.

ALSO BY CARL HIAASEN

Tourist Season	Sick Puppy
Double Whammy	Basket Case
Skin Tight	Skinny Dip
Native Tongue	Nature Girl
Strip Tease	Star Island
Stormy Weather	Bad Monkey
Lucky You	Razor Girl

With William Montalbano

A Death in China
Trap Line
Powder Burn

For young readers

Hoot
Flush
Scat
Chomp
Skink

Nonfiction

Paradise Screwed: Selected Columns
(edited by Diane Stevenson)

Kick Ass: Selected Columns
(edited by Diane Stevenson)

Team Rodent: How Disney Devours the World

The Downhill Lie: A Hacker's Return
to a Ruinous Sport

Dance of the Reptiles: Selected Columns
(edited by Diane Stevenson)

*

Also by Roz Chast

Going into Town
Can't We Talk About Something More Pleasant?
The Party, After You Left
What I Hate: From A to Z
Theories of Everything

ASSUME THE WORST

The Graduation Speech You'll Never Hear

Carl Hiaasen

ILLUSTRATED BY
Roz Chast

sphere

SPHERE

First published in the United States in 2018 by
Alfred A. Knopf, a division of Penguin Random House, LLC.
First published in Great Britain in 2018 by Sphere

10 9 8 7 6 5 4 3 2 1

Copyright © Carl Hiaasen 2018
Illusrations copyright © Roz Chast 2018

The moral right of the author has been asserted.

All rights reserved.
No part of this publication may be reproduced, stored in a retrieval
system, or transmitted, in any form or by any means, without the
prior permission in writing of the publisher, nor be otherwise
circulated in any form of binding or cover other than that in
which it is published and without a similar condition including
this condition being imposed on the subsequent purchaser.

A CIP catalogue record for this book is available from the British Library.

ISBN 978-0-7515-7416-6

Printed and bound by CPI Group (UK) Ltd, Croydon, CR0 4YY

Papers used by Sphere are from well-managed forests
and other responsible sources.

Sphere
An imprint of
Little, Brown Book Group
Carmelite House
50 Victoria Embankment
London EC4Y 0DZ

An Hachette UK Company
www.hachette.co.uk

www.littlebrown.co.uk

*For Quinn,
soaring off to college*

ASSUME THE WORST

This commencement address will never be given, because graduation speakers are supposed to offer encouragement and inspiration.

That's not what you need. You need a warning.

After an uncommonly long career observing and writing about misbehavior,

ASSUME THE WORST

I have one piece of advice as you launch yourselves from college: Assume the worst.

Based on the last six thousand years of human history, it's the only sensible way to proceed. Lowering your expectations will inoculate you against serial disappointments. It will also set you up for heart-lifting surprises on those occasions when someone you meet turns out to be unexpectedly honorable, generous and selfless.

If I were actually standing at a podium, looking out at a sea of young hope-filled faces, I'd begin with a raw appraisal of the real world: It's pretty fucked up.

It was fucked up when I graduated, too, but not this bad. Our vernacular contained no

[3]

such terms as "active shooter," "ISIS-inspired" or "viral cat video."

Still, I'd bet that even the brightest of you would sit there thinking—as past generations have—okay, it's *got* to get better.

ASSUME THE WORST

I'm here to say: No, it doesn't.

And where did you get such a tender idea?

The day I got out of college, in 1974, a vainglorious paranoid was in the White House, shredding the U.S. Constitution for toilet paper. There was a futile and tragic overseas war, hatred and bloodshed in the Middle East, dissent and injustice on the streets of America.

Ring a bell?

The forces of indifference, incompetence and evil—yup, it exists—are thriving in the twenty-first century. No matter what good things you try to do, you're in for a slog.

I'm not saying you shouldn't dream of

[5]

making an impact. Just understand that the odds are stacked against you.

One key to meaningful achievement is disregarding the lame platitudes you'll hear in real commencement speeches, group therapy and self-help podcasts:

ASSUME THE WORST

1. Live each day as if it's your last.

As wise and appealing as this might sound, it's actually terrible advice. If you live every day as if it's your last, you won't accomplish a damn thing. You'll soon run out of money, your car will get repossessed, you'll be evicted from your apartment, and the person you're living with will dump you for somebody with a mid-level management job at BrandsMart.

Spending all your waking hours doing only what feels good is a viable life plan if you're a Labrador retriever, but for humans it's a blueprint for unemployment, divorce and irrelevance.

ASSUME THE WORST

Even if you love your job, there's no such thing as a carefree life. Most of you will one day awake in a cold sweat realizing those noisy little people in the bedroom down the hall totally depend on you. They're called

[9]

children. You'll cherish them more than anything and worry about them forever, even when they're all grown up and wiping the applesauce off your bib at the nursing home.

When Charles Darwin laid out his theory

of evolution, he famously concluded that natural selection relies on the "survival of the fittest." Well, the fittest of any advanced species survive mainly because they worry. The nervous caveman who insisted on sleeping near the campfire made it through the night alive. His carefree pal who strung up a hammock in the dark jungle got eaten by the saber-toothed tiger.

That, in a bloody nutshell, is the story of our gene pool.

2. If you set your mind to it, you can be anything you want to be.

Total bullshit. Nobody can be absolutely anything they want to be—no matter how

I'm an old cowhand from 2921 West 745th Street.
Yippee-yi-don't-think-so.

ASSUME THE WORST

hard they wish, pray or try. I wanted to play major-league baseball like Willie Mays but, unfortunately, I couldn't run, catch or hit like Willie Mays. And I *tried*. Really hard. By eighth grade I'd bagged the whole fantasy and moved on.

Self-delusion is no virtue. Anyone who tells you the sky's the limit is blowing smoke up your ass. That's not to say you can't achieve something remarkable and enduring. But doing that will be impossible if you fail to grasp your own strengths and weaknesses. In other words, work with what you've got.

If Bill Gates had set out to be, say, a professional bronco rider, he wouldn't have made it past his first rodeo. He would have

been catapulted from the saddle, stomped senseless by his horse, and "Microsoft" would today be a brand of absorbent underwear.

The most successful and productive people recognize their own talent and find a way to uncork it. Of course, such keen

ASSUME THE WORST

self-awareness can cut both ways. Bruce Springsteen knew he'd be good at writing songs. Bernie Madoff, on the other hand, knew he'd be good at embezzling.

Strive to excel at something that won't get you indicted. Prison sucks.

3. Try to find goodness in everyone you meet.

Another waste of time. Relationships aren't supposed to be reclamation projects. The humane qualities of any new acquaintance should be evident in the first five minutes of conversation—ten minutes, tops.

If it requires the psychological equivalent of a metal detector to locate somebody's true self, then they're not worth the trouble. Life is short. Say good-bye.

None of you in this imaginary throng needs to be told there's a glut of assholes on the loose. You went to school with some of them, and guess what? They'll never change.

ASSUME THE WORST

If you don't believe me now, send me a text after your ten-year class reunion.

These days we all need a default Asshole-Avoidance mode, to help navigate around people who are intractably arrogant, greedy, conniving or cruel. The ability to sidestep and outwit these random jerks is a necessary skill. If you don't know how, you'd better learn.

Corruption is another dreary fact of life, and the worst scoundrels are often likable and smooth. Try not to fall for their act. From the local zoning board to the halls of Congress, your mistrust will seldom be misplaced.

ASSUME THE WORST

4. Don't be quick to judge others.

Are you kidding? If you don't learn how to judge others—and judge fast—you'll get metaphorically trampled from now until the day you die.

All of you fictitious future grads were quickly judged before being accepted by this institution, just as you'll be quickly judged in your upcoming job interviews. Your future colleagues will judge you, your future loan officers will judge you and your future spouse's family will judge you. Get used to it, and tune yourselves to judge back.

Sharpen an aptitude for cold-eyed discernment. Selecting friends, lovers and business

ASSUME THE WORST

partners are important decisions. It's all right to prefer honest, alert, intelligent people.

Stupidity is a real-world pandemic from which there's no refuge, even at college. Each year, on prestigious campuses from coast to coast, no small number of diplomas are handed out to young men and women who barely scraped by.

And that's how they'll conduct their adulthoods, barely scraping by.

Being less than smart doesn't automatically make you stupid. In this era that label should be reserved for those who are doggedly reckless, defiantly uninformed or proactively disconnected.

For instance, you all know people who proudly refuse to accept—despite the tonnage of scientific evidence—that the earth's climate is changing. Arctic ice caps puddle, equatorial oceans rise, subtropical deserts grow hotter,

yet these chowderheads claim it's all a political lie, fake news.

And they'll tell you that while they're standing ankle-deep in tidewater on a street corner in Miami Beach.

During prehistoric times, such blundering specimens would have made an easy supper for the fleet and the fanged. Today, in the absence of feral predators, the unfittest survive longer and cause more damage.

Many of them find their way to voting booths on Election Day. Your duty is to offset the harm they do by making sure that you, too, vote. This will require staying minimally aware of current events, and showing up before the polls close.

When that doesn't happen—when the ignorant outperform the attentive—dimness triumphs. The result is that we end up with dangerously unqualified leaders, and then sit around disconsolately hoping the worst of them will be taken down by scandal, or maybe an exploding prostate.

Such crises can be averted if a majority of you pay attention. It helps to be equipped with actual facts, which are almost never acquired from memes, chat rooms or talk radio.

Society has been deeply divided before, but never has it been so inanely distracted. Don't be shocked if more Americans can

ASSUME THE WORST

identify all the Kardashian sisters than can find Serbia on a world map.

It's hard to say whether humankind in totality is dumber today than it was back in 1974, but there's no question that more dumb behavior is on wider display.

If I were speaking to a live college audience, I'd have everyone take out their phones and find something breathlessly idiotic that's been posted this morning on Instagram or Facebook. Within moments you'd be sharing video of some drunk shooting a bottle rocket out of his butt—or possibly a compilation of drunks shooting bottle rockets out of their butts, perhaps set to a chorus of "The Battle Hymn of the Republic."

Darwin would be fascinated by the streaming anthropology of social media. It's a geyser of ominous evidence that our species has begun to de-evolve, receding back to the slime bog from which we first emerged as gasping, bug-eyed salamanders.

So far, our legacy contribution as citizen organisms is mayhem. We're plundering and poisoning the planet with way more gusto than our long-ago ancestors did, while we torment and slaughter one another just as wantonly—and with record body counts.

Technology is all that's changed. We're much more efficient at carnage now. Try your very hardest not to participate.

At this point in my pretend graduation

ASSUME THE WORST

speech, you'd probably be shifting in your seats and thinking: *Wow. Life is a total shit blizzard, and we're all fucking doomed.*

Yes, life is a shit blizzard. No, you're not all doomed.

Assuming the worst is the best and most promising course. It will keep despair and disillusionment at bay. It will also free you to be pleasantly startled when you get a boss who's actually good at his or her job, meet a politician who can't be bought off by lobbyists, or dine with a twitchy in-law who doesn't hit you up for money.

At such moments, hope is allowed. So is wary idealism.

HOPE
I have a feeling he's not an ignorant sleazeball!
And I am entertaining the possibility that she is not a self-serving weasel!

ASSUME THE WORST

The profession I chose—journalism—wouldn't exist if young people didn't believe change was possible, even in the most harrowing and soul-sapping of times.

I skipped my own graduation ceremony because the small newspaper that had hired me expected me to show up for work. Then, as now, the only excusable reason for becoming a reporter was to expose things that were wrong and unjust, on the slim chance that somebody in authority might do something about it.

Once in a while they actually did. And it happened just often enough to keep me from seeking another line of work.

Which leads to the part of the commencement address when every speaker feels obliged to talk about happiness. Where do you find it? How do you sustain it?

I haven't got a clue. If you're searching for

ASSUME THE WORST

a spiritual pathway to serenity, ask your yoga teacher. Or maybe buy a puppy.

Here's all I know about happiness: It's slippery. It's unpredictable. It's a different sensation for everyone.

But one thing happiness is *not* is overrated. When you luck into some, enjoy every minute.

Grandparents of my generation were fond of telling us to "spread a little happiness wherever you go." For some of you it will be easier to spread the flu.

ASSUME THE WORST

Happiness can't be sprinkled around like fairy dust. By disposition some folks are more contented than others, but none of us glides along in a cloud of perpetual bliss.

People who are truly hurting are grateful for one happy moment. All it takes to bring them a smile—or maybe a laugh—is a single act of comfort.

For many of you, reaching out to help will be a moral reflex. To those who must be reminded to behave that way, let me say this: Your parents dropped the ball, big-time. Force yourself to experiment with kindness, even when the impulse eludes you.

If I were speaking to actual graduates, I could look out over the crowd and predict

with absolute certainty that some of you
are blessed with monster talent, and you'll
do amazing things. You won't change the
whole world, but you'll change *somebody's*
world—and for the better.

And, just as inevitably, some of you won't.
You'll park your principles in the long-term
lot and spend your future taking advantage of
people. Others of you, burdened with a deficit
of ambition, won't do much of anything.
You could easily end up working in a robocall
center, peddling shitty insurance policies to
senior citizens.

At the other end of the productivity
spectrum, those of you who own a functioning conscience, a sturdy set of values and

ASSUME THE WORST

a tolerance for hard work ought to do just fine. You deserve many happy moments.

If you set your mind to it, you can be lots of things, but not the next Willie Mays, a champion bronco rider or even an acoustic shadow of Bruce Springsteen.

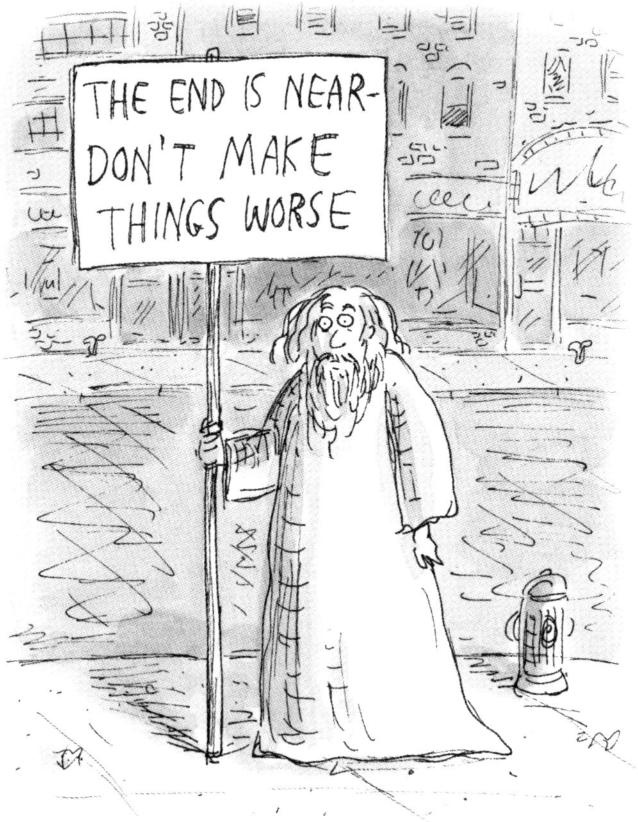
THE END IS NEAR-
DON'T MAKE
THINGS WORSE

ASSUME THE WORST

To sum up:

Figure out what you're good at, and get better at it. Along the way, don't waste your time on people whose decency isn't apparent when you first meet for a cup of coffee. Be an astute judge of character, and learn to judge quickly.

Read the news. Pay attention. Always aspire to act in a way that cancels out someone else's cruel or stupid behavior.

Never stop worrying. Live each day as if your rent is due tomorrow.

And always, *always* be the one who sleeps near the campfire—the one who would make Darwin proud.

Our Ancestors

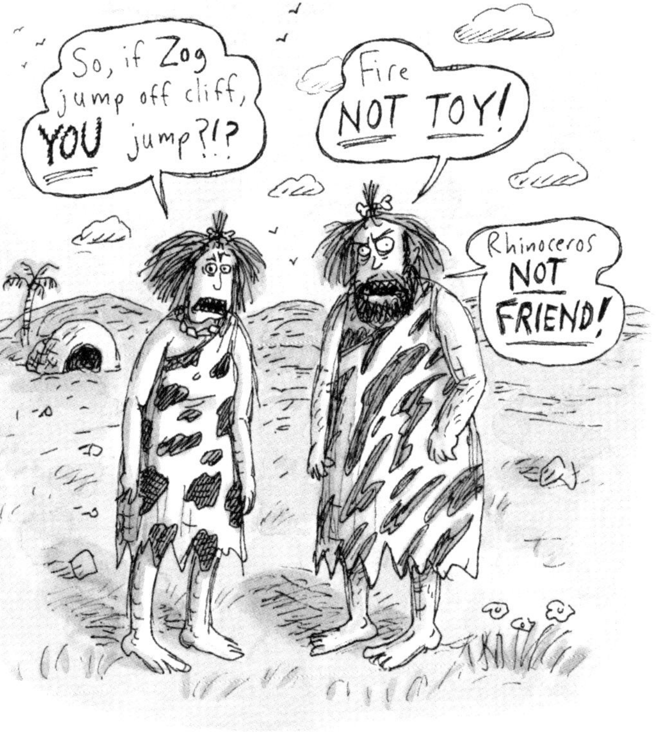

SHORTLISTED FOR THE BOLLINGER EVERYMAN
WODEHOUSE PRIZE 2017

**Key West is a small place, but there are criminal
secrets buried everywhere ...**

When jumped-up reality TV star Buck Nance aggravates
the crowd in a Key West bar, he incites a riot and vanishes in the
melee. His hapless agent Lane Coolman should have been by
Buck's side, but has been accidentally taken hostage by two petty
criminals who now think they can turn a quick profit by
ransoming an LA talent agent.

As the search for Buck continues, the mystery draws
in a broad cast of characters from across the island including
Andrew Yancy, the disgraced cop who now works restaurants on
roach patrol; a delusional fan of Buck's show; the local sheriff who's
desperate for re-election; a shady lawyer and his gold-digging
fiancée; the gay mayor and his restauranteur partner; a Mafioso
hotelier; and a redheaded con artist named Merry who, using a
razor blade and a high-speed car, has developed a signature
way of luring in her victims.

'Poetic justice and social satire are hallmarks of Carl Hiaasen's
work and *Razor Girl* deals out both in fine fashion'
New Zealand Listener

When a severed arm is discovered by a couple on honeymoon in the Florida Keys, former police detective – now reluctant restaurant inspector – Andrew Yancy senses that something doesn't add up. Determined to get his badge back, he undertakes an unofficial investigation of his own.

Andrew's search for the truth takes him to the Bahamas, where a local man, with the help of a very bad monkey (who allegedly worked on the *Pirates of the Caribbean* movies) is doing everything in his power to prevent a developer from building a new tourist resort on the island, with deadly consequences …

'Vintage Hiaasen … Hilarious madcap fun'
Daily Express

'The funniest crime novelist to put pen to paper'
Evening Standard

CARL
HIAASEN
STAR ISLAND

Twenty-two-year-old pop star Cherry Pye is attempting a comeback from her latest drug-fuelled disaster. Her 'stunt double' Ann travels everywhere with her, throwing paparazzi off the scent when they get too close.

But one night, Ann's resemblance to Cherry Pye proves too convincing – she is kidnapped by an obsessed paparazzo who only realises his mistake once it is too late to go back . . .

'Exhilarating return to form for the satirical Florida crime writer . . . a witty satire and a nail-biting thriller'
The Times

'Is there a funnier novelist on the planet than Carl Hiaasen? I hope not, because after nearly injuring myself reading his latest comic thriller I don't think my poor body could take it'
Mail on Sunday